CONIFERS

CONIFERS

AN ILLUSTRATED GUIDE TO VARIETIES, CULTIVATION AND CARE, WITH STEP-BY-STEP INSTRUCTIONS AND OVER 160 BEAUTIFUL PHOTOGRAPHS

Andrew Mikolajski

Consultant: Colin Morgan
Photography by Peter Anderson

southwater

This edition is published by Southwater
an imprint of Anness Publishing Ltd
Blaby Road, Wigston, Leicestershire LE18 4SE
info@anness.com

www.southwaterbooks.com; www.annesspublishing.com

A CIP catalogue record for this book is available from the British Library.

Publisher: Joanna Lorenz
Senior Editor: Clare Nicholson
Designer: Michael Morey
Production Controller: Pirong Wang

Contents

Introduction

Plant Directory

The Grower's Guide

Introduction

Conifers are among the most fascinating of plants. They are a diverse group ranging from mighty giants, such as the redwoods, to dwarfs suitable for rock and scree gardens, troughs and windowboxes. Mainly evergreen, tough and hardy, conifers give year-round pleasure, providing superb backdrops to the transient flowers of summer, then coming into their own in autumn and winter as their firm outlines begin to dominate the scene. Conifers occur in a wide range of colours, from blue-grey through many shades of green to golden yellow. This book explains the place of conifers in the plant kingdom, suggests ways in which they can be used in the garden, and illustrates some of the most striking now in cultivation.

■ RIGHT

Mature conifers are magnificent trees, here a fine specimen of the Dawn redwood (*Metasequoia glyptostroboides*) dominates a pool-side planting.

Conifers in garden history

■ BELOW
Conifers develop a range of habits, including upright, conical and spreading.

Conifers are mainly evergreen trees that occur widely throughout the forested regions of the temperate and sub-tropical world. They are distinguished from other trees by producing their seed in cones rather than fruits and from other evergreens by having, in the main, needle-like leaves. Exceptions are the larches (*Larix*), the Swamp or Bald cypress (*Taxodium*) and the Dawn redwood (*Metasequoia*), all of which are deciduous. Cypresses (*Cupressus*) and junipers (*Juniperus*) have scale-like leaves; *Podocarpus* and *Agathis*, both of which include tender species, have thin, broad, flattened leaves. The Maidenhair tree (*Ginkgo biloba*), not strictly a conifer, more a living fossil, is often included among them. It is distantly related to the conifers but has fan-shaped leaves that are shed in autumn and produces fleshy fruits. (For further details on conifer characteristics and nomenclature, see Conifer botany.)

Conifers are primitive plants, many of which have survived since prehistoric times without further evolution. The Maidenhair tree and Dawn redwood are known from fossilized remains – indeed the latter was thought extinct until its rediscovery in China in 1947. The conifer group also includes the oldest, tallest and smallest trees on the planet. Specimens of the Bristle cone pine (*Pinus aristata*), from Arizona, New Mexico and Colorado, are estimated to be nearly 5,000 years old. Also from the New World, the Coastal redwood (*Sequoia sempervirens*) is the tallest tree at 112m (367ft), while its close relative, the Giant redwood (*Sequoiadendron giganteum*), is the largest by mass. The smallest conifer, from New Zealand, is *Lepidothamnus laxifolius,* which grows no higher than 8cm (3in).

Many conifers are grown commercially throughout the

■ LEFT
A planting of conifers that includes two "Christmas trees".

temperate world for their timber, oils and resins. Conifer wood is classified as softwood, unlike that of deciduous trees, which is termed hardwood. Some conifers, however, do produce very hard wood. Douglas fir, pine, redwood and juniper are widely used by the construction industry for building and fencing. Spruce, pine, fir and hemlock are grown to produce wood pulp for paper manufacture. Pine wood is resinous and has been widely used in the production of rosin, pitch, turpentine, varnishes and lacquers (though today these are often also made synthetically). Oils from conifers hold a significant place in complementary medicine and in the manufacture of woody-based perfumes – firs, cedars and pines being particularly important.

Pine kernels are edible raw, and are an essential ingredient of *pesto* sauce. Juniper berries, also edible, are used in the production of gin.

Some conifers are grown for cutting as Christmas trees, the most popular being the quick-growing Norway spruce (*Picea abies*). The Noble fir (*Abies procera*), Caucasian fir (*Abies nordmanniana*) and the Scots pine (*Pinus sylvestris*) are gaining in popularity because of their needle-holding characteristics. The Monkey puzzle (*Araucaria*) is sometimes used in warm climates.

The ancient Egyptians used resins from the Aleppo pine (*Pinus halepensis*), the Cilician fir (*Abies cilicica*) and the Caucasian spruce (*Picea orientalis*) for embalming and some woods for tomb furnishings. Several types were planted as shade

■ BELOW LEFT
Conifers and heathers are natural allies and provide a long season of interest.

■ BELOW RIGHT
Hardwood and softwood: Silver birch and cypress.

■ LEFT
A number of species now grown in gardens come from the mountains of North America.

trees in the later civilization of Mesopotamia. King Tiglath-Pileser I (1114–1026 BC) introduced the cedar – probably the biblical Cedar of Lebanon (*Cedrus libani*) – into Assyria. Other conifers cultivated there included cypresses and junipers. Chinese emperors planted *Platycladus orientalis* in front of their tombs to protect them in the spirit world.

In ancient Greece conifers such as the Italian or Mediterranean cypress (*Cupressus sempervirens*), the Aleppo pine, the Umbrella or Stone pine (*Pinus pinea*) and the Grecian fir (*Abies cephalonica*) were valued as shade plants and used with planes, oaks and poplars for walkways. In the 1st century AD, the Roman letter-writer, Pliny the Younger, advocated using conifers in a formalized way, planting them in straight rows.

The role of conifers in medieval gardens is a matter of conjecture, but Pliny's ideas were revived in Renaissance Italy. Conifers were also put to similar use in the geometric gardens of Islam. The 12th-century Arab botanist In al-Awwam, writing of gardens in Spain, recommended using cypresses to mark corners and growing them with cedars and pines in rows to make shaded walkways.

The Italian cypress reached Britain at the end of the 14th century, and the biblical Cedar of Lebanon arrived in the 17th. The 17th-century diarist John Evelyn recommended using yew for topiary; among the other conifers he mentioned were the Italian cypress, the Cedar of Lebanon, the Stone or Umbrella pine, the Norway spruce, the Silver fir (*Abies alba*) and the larch (*Larix decidua*). Plant-hunting in Asia produced a male Maidenhair tree (*Ginkgo biloba*), brought to Europe from China in 1730; the specimen survives in Kew Gardens, England.

The discovery and colonization of the New World significantly widened the range of plants available to European gardeners. In the 17th century the English plant collector John Tradescant the Younger brought back the Swamp or Bald cypress (*Taxodium distichum*). Other newcomers were the White cedar (*Thuja occidentalis*) and the Weymouth or White pine (*Pinus strobus*). The Rev. John Banister sent the Balsam fir (*Abies balsamea*) to England from Virginia in the 18th century. Towards the end of that century came the Labrador or Jack pine (*Pinus banksiana*). Other American introductions were the Pencil cedar (*Juniperus virginiana*) and the Virginian pine and Pitch pine (*Pinus virginiana* and *P. rigida*).

Conifers became important in Europe in the 18th century with the vogue for the English style of landscape gardening, in which stands of trees were planted to mark focal points or frame a vista. The Scots pine (*Pinus sylvestris*) was a favourite for this purpose, with exotic imports such as cedars and the Swamp cypress. With the contemporary passion for collecting, grand gardens of the period often included "plantations", large plantings of trees and shrubs in serried ranks, large at the back, small at the front; among the evergreens were conifers, both native and foreign. Many of the North American introductions proved hard to establish, being lime-hating, and adapted to hotter summers and colder winters. At the end of the century, this led to the creation – frequently at vast expense – of special "American" gardens with the boggy, acid soil in which the imported conifers could thrive. These gardens were later used to grow other lime-hating plants such as Himalayan rhododendrons and *Pieris*.

In the 19th century it became fashionable to devote a section of the garden to a pinetum, a collection exclusively of coniferous plants. Around the middle of the century the Monkey puzzle (*Araucaria araucana*) became popular. Introduced from Chile by Archibald Menzies in 1795 (it is also found in Argentina), it became widely available only when seed was collected in 1844.

Adrian Bloom has been one of the keenest advocates of conifers in garden design in the 20th century, and has introduced many of the dwarf cultivars suitable for today's smaller gardens. He also developed the island bed – to be viewed from more than one side, unlike the traditional herbaceous border – in which conifers play a dominant role.

Nowadays, conifers are found in all kinds of gardens, from large country estates to small town gardens.

BOTTOM LEFT
Moisture-loving conifers planted as a background to a water garden; *Gunnera* is in the foreground with *Eupatorium* behind.

BOTTOM RIGHT
An elegant conifer lifts the eye above transient summer herbaceous perennials.

Conifers in the garden

Conifers are essential in the garden, providing year-round interest. They are effective as foils to the more opulent plants of spring and summer, but come into their own when the flower-beds are bare in winter and their shapes, textures and colours become dominant. Site them with care, for then they become the bones of the garden. Aim for harmony of shape and contour whether you opt for a formal or informal scheme. With heights ranging from 90cm (3ft) for a dwarf conifer, such as *Picea pungens* 'Globosa', to the 90m (300ft) or more of the Giant redwood, and a variety of colours, there is a conifer for every garden situation.

■ ABOVE
A planting that demonstrates the range of colours and shapes offered by conifers.

■ LEFT
A dumpy dwarf conifer squats next to a candelabra-like tree heath.

GOLDEN-LEAVED CONIFERS

Chamaecyparis lawsoniana 'Lanei'
Chamaecyparis lawsoniana 'Stewartii'
x *Cupressocyparis leylandii* 'Castlewellan'
Cupressus macrocarpa 'Goldcrest'
Juniperus chinensis 'Aurea'
Pinus sylvestris 'Aurea'
Thuja plicata 'Zebrina'

■ BOTTOM LEFT
Conifers here make a striking foil to bamboo and golden-leaved elder.

■ LEFT
A collection of large conifers makes a magisterial statement in the depths of winter.

■ BOTTOM RIGHT
The sun lights up the golden leaves of the conifer seen against the striking foliage of *Gunnera manicata.*

You are often best able to appreciate the beauties of individual conifers during quiet spells in the gardening year. Many have decorative cones. Those of the Korean fir (*Abies koreana*) are a striking violet-blue, while those of the Macedonian pine (*Pinus peuce*) exude white resin. *Pinus bungeana* has decorative bark, richly deserving its common name Lace-bark pine. The bark flakes off to reveal creamy patches that darken to purplish-grey and then grey-green. Some cultivars of the Japanese cedar (*Cryptomeria japonica*) that retain the juvenile foliage redden dramatically in winter. All deciduous conifers have good autumn colour.

Glaucous (blue-green) conifers develop their most intense leaf colour in cold, frosty weather. Conversely, those with yellow leaves produce the best colour on new growth in early spring, when the garden is re-awakening after winter.

If you have a very large garden, consider planting a collection of conifers as a pinetum (or mix them with broad-leaved trees), arranging them by their country of origin or family group. Dwarf forms are best planted away from larger specimens that may cast too much shade over them. In a small garden you could create a miniature pinetum using dwarf conifers, such as *Pinus mugo* 'Corley's Mat', *Picea abies* 'Gregoryana', *Thuja plicata* 'Irish Gold' or *Tsuga canadensis* 'Jeddeloh'.

Where space permits exciting effects can be created by combining and contrasting different tree shapes, for instance planting the columnar *Chamaecyparis lawsoniana* 'Green

■ LEFT
Two trees for water-logged soil. The widely grown Weeping willow is an effective stablemate for the elegant Dawn redwood.

Pillar' with a prostrate juniper such as *Juniperus procumbens* or *J. squamata* 'Holger'. Others are best allowed to make their own statement as specimen trees in grass or gravel. In a large garden the Cedar of Lebanon could be a first choice. Equally handsome are its relatives the Atlas cedar (*Cedrus atlantica*), which has handsome, fissured bark, the magnificent blue form, *C.a.* f. *glauca,* or the Deodar (*Cedrus deodara*) from the Himalayas. The Maidenhair tree is also a good choice as are the spruces *Picea breweriana* and *P. omorika* and the Western hemlock (*Tsuga heterophylla*). The Japanese cedar makes a striking obelisk shape.

■ ABOVE RIGHT
A mature conifer dominates the skyline and gives the garden interest and shape.

■ BELOW
A golden-leaved conifer glows in the winter sun.

In a smaller space *Cupressus macrocarpa* 'Goldcrest' or the equally decorative *Chamaecyparis pisifera* 'Filifera Aurea' may fit the bill. By water, try one of the moisture-loving deciduous conifers, either *Taxodium* or *Metasequoia.* Both provide a brilliant blaze of orange and red in autumn.

Conifers can also be planted effectively in avenues. The upright Irish yew (*Taxus baccata* 'Fastigiata') is probably the best for this purpose and can be wired to make an even more formal shape. Other possibilities are *Juniperus communis* 'Hibernica' and *J. virginiana* 'Blue Arrow'. *J. v.* 'Skyrocket', once widely grown for this purpose, is no longer recommended since it tends to die

■ BOTTOM
Dwarf conifers planted in proximity meld into an organic whole.

back after a number of years. Longer-living, newer cultivars have superseded it.

Dwarf conifers planted close together will grow into each other, assuming a sculptural quality, besides making excellent ground cover. Some form dense mats, particularly the prostrate junipers such as *Juniperus horizontalis, J. squamata* and *J. procumbens*; all have many cultivars. *Taxus baccata* 'Repens Aurea' is another candidate. Most dwarfs are suitable for rock gardens, and containers. Other conifers for containers are *Cupressus macrocarpa* 'Goldcrest', *C. sempervirens* 'Stricta' and *Juniperus communis* 'Compressa'.

Some conifers have specialized applications in the garden. Rapid growers such as x *Cupressocyparis leylandii* make useful barrier plantings in a large garden and can act as windbreaks, either grown as hedges or mixed with other plants such as hollies (see Conifer hedges). A few conifers can be clipped for topiary – yew is the most widely used (see Pruning). For complementary plantings, conifers and heathers are natural allies. Choose upright conifers which help to punctuate and break up the even mass of a heather bed. You can also use conifers as host plants for summer-flowering climbers such as clematis or climbing roses.

GLAUCOUS-LEAVED CONIFERS

Cedrus atlantica f. *glauca*
Chamaecyparis lawsoniana 'Pembury Blue'
Cupressus glabra 'Pyramidalis'
Tsuga mertensiana f. *argentea*

Conifer botany

■ RIGHT
Needle-like leaves arranged spirally along a stem.

Conifers belong to a division in the plant kingdom called gymnosperms – plants that produce naked seed (from the Greek *gymnos* meaning "naked", and *sperma*, "seed"). Other gymnosperms include palms and cycads. Conifers are assumed to be "lower" or more primitive plants than the angiosperms (flowering plants), which produce covered seed.

Conifers and other gymnosperms do not flower in the conventional sense. In spring, the male and female cones appear together with new shoots and leaves, though they may not be conspicuous. At this stage they are sometimes referred to botanically as *strobili*. The males ripen and shed their pollen grains, then wither and drop. Pollination is effected by the wind, which blows the pollen on to the sticky surface of the female cone's ovule (the structure on which fertilization takes place). The female cone develops as a woody structure, the scales of which part to release the ripe seed, a few months to two and a half years after pollination, depending on the species. Conifer seed usually has a papery "wing" attached to it, and it is also wind-borne.

Juniper berries are carried profusely on mature plants. They are used in the making of gin and dried for culinary use.

The cones of the Korean fir are a striking violet-blue initially and age to brown. They can be borne on young plants.

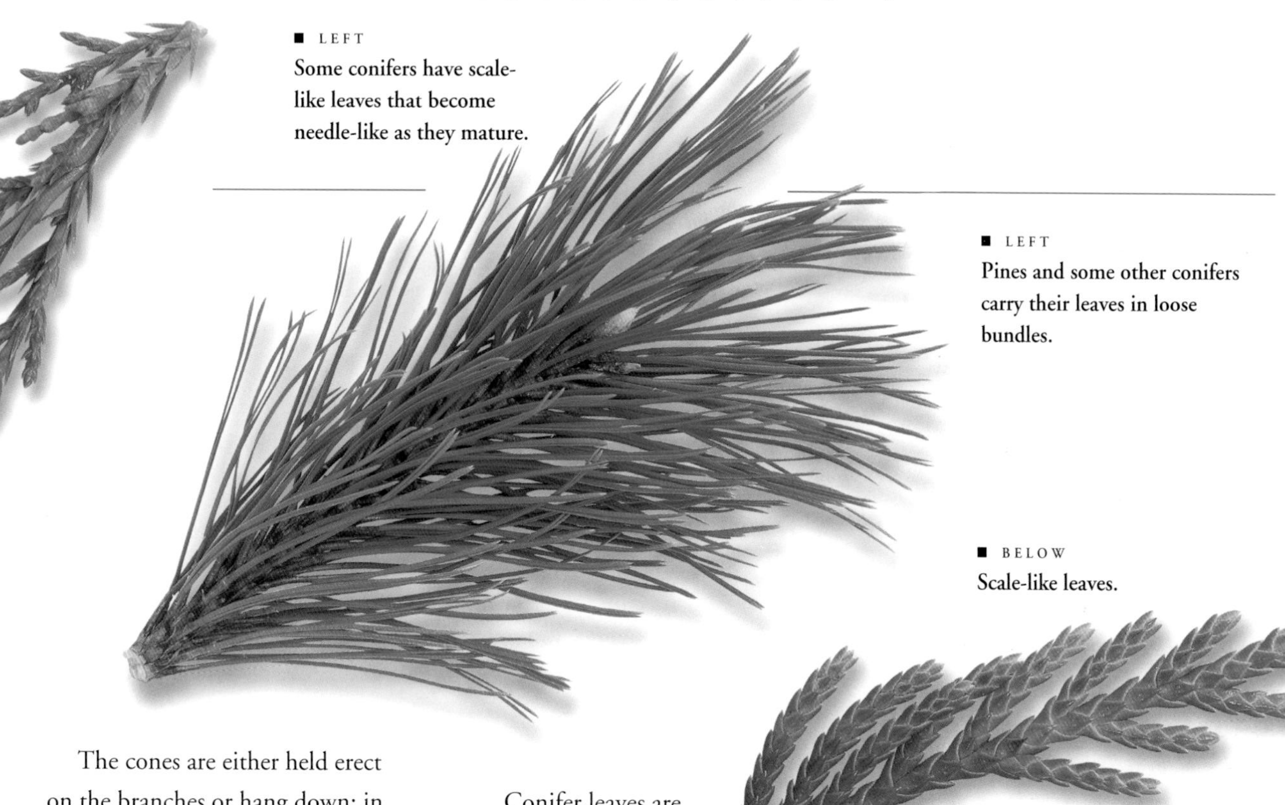

■ LEFT
Some conifers have scale-like leaves that become needle-like as they mature.

■ LEFT
Pines and some other conifers carry their leaves in loose bundles.

■ BELOW
Scale-like leaves.

The cones are either held erect on the branches or hang down; in many cases the female cones are conspicuous and a decorative feature. Male and female cones may be borne on separate plants (such species are described botanically as dioecious), or may be produced on the same plant (monoecious). In the case of yew (*Taxus*) and juniper (*Juniperus*), however, the cones are modified into fleshy, berry-like structures. The Nutmeg yew (*Torreya*) also produces berry-like fruits. The "berry" of the yew is cup-like and open-ended, which means the seed is still naked. In the wild the berries are eaten by birds and animals and the seed is not wind-borne, so these genera are assumed to be more highly evolved than other conifers.

Conifer leaves are usually needle-like (botanically, linear or acicular), or scale-like. Some species of *Podocarpus* and all *Agathis*, however, produce broader, flattened needle-like leaves. The leaves may be carried in two ranks opposite each other on the stem in a comb-like arrangement. In some cases they are in whorls (a circular arrangement of three or more arising from a single point). Sometimes, they are borne spirally along stems or in loose bundles. Spruces (*Picea*) have leaves that are set singly but densely,

■ BELOW
Conifer leaves can be carried in two ranks in a comb-like arrangement.

■ RIGHT
The seeds of most conifers have papery "wings" and are dispersed by the wind.

resulting in bristly branches in some species. Most conifer leaves are stiff and hard, and they have a waxy surface that prevents evaporation, a form of protection essential to the plant's survival in freezing conditions. They are usually mid- to dark green, but some are yellowish and others have a glaucous bloom that makes them appear blue, silver or grey.

Conifer genes are unstable, and different cultivars of the same species can be of widely divergent size, habit and growth rate. Most are strongly upright, naturally forming tall, slim obelisks or cone shapes. Many, such as the Scots pine, become more spreading as they mature, forming a broad crown. A few, such as the Kashmir cypress (*Cupressus torulosa* 'Cashmeriana'), have pendulous, weeping branches. A few conifers, however, are prostrate plants that hug the ground. Some dwarf forms make dense mounds or cone shapes.

Many conifers are resinous and have sticky, aromatic stems. Though some are so well-clothed with foliage that the central trunk is barely visible, if at all, others shed their lower branches as they mature and develop a characteristic head. In some cases the bark is striking. The Black pine (*Pinus jeffreyi*) for instance, has greyish shoots and black bark that is deeply fissured (split). The Patagonian cypress (*Fitzroya cupressoides*) has reddish-brown bark that peels in strips. The Chinese fir (*Cunninghamia lanceolata*) also has distinctive, fibrous, red-brown bark.

Changes in nomenclature (the system by which plants are named) have resulted in some potential confusion. Certain common names have persisted while botanical divisions have altered. Not all conifers

Some conifers shed their lower branches naturally as they mature and then develop a characteristic crown.

■ LEFT
Cones, in a range of sizes, split open to release the seed.

■ LEFT
The bark of some conifers is fibrous and peeling.

commonly referred to as cedars belong to the genus *Cedrus*: botanically, the Japanese cedar is *Cryptomeria japonica*, the White cedar *Thuja occidentalis*. The Swamp cypress belongs to *Taxodium* not *Cupressus*. The so-called Japanese umbrella pine is actually *Sciadopitys verticillata*. Nor are all firs *Abies*: some belong to *Pseudotsuga*.

■ ABOVE
The deeply furrowed bark of the Dawn redwood.

■ FAR LEFT
The bark of *Chamaecyparis lawsoniana* forms woody, scaly plates that lift at the edges.

■ LEFT
Some conifers have bark that peels off in long strips.

Plant Directory

Large conifers

In the following directory, conifers are grouped according to their mature size.

Large conifers exceed 15m (50ft) when mature, many being considerably taller. Medium-sized conifers achieve a height of between 10–15m (33–50ft). Small and dwarf conifers generally do not exceed 10m (33ft); many are considerably smaller.

The heights and spreads given here are what the trees may be expected to achieve given good cultivation, though some are slow-growing and may take many decades to reach their final height. Owing to the longevity of conifers, in many cases the ultimate height cannot be accurately predicted. Growth rates will vary depending on the soil type, local climate and prevailing conditions.

Unless otherwise stated, all the conifers described here grow best in fertile, well-drained soil in sun or partial shade. They will withstand temperatures of -15°C (5°F); some are considerably hardier. All are evergreen and assumed to be monoecious. All cones described are female.

■ ABOVE

ABIES GRANDIS (GIANT FIR, GRAND FIR)

Larger conifer from west North America that grows into a tall, slim cone-shaped tree. The needle-like leaves are dark green banded with white beneath, and smell of oranges when they are crushed. The cones ripen from green to reddish brown. Height to 60m (approx. 200ft), spread to 8m (26ft). Vigorous but elegant, the Giant fir is a good choice where a handsome specimen is needed quickly.

■ ABOVE
ABIES PROCERA (SYN. *A. NOBILIS*) (NOBLE FIR)

Large conifer from the USA that forms a cone-shaped tree, maturing to a broader, irregular obelisk. The needle-like leaves are arranged in two ranks and turn up sharply from the base; they are greyish green and sometimes have a glaucous cast. Mature trees have silvery-grey, fissured bark; the cones are green. Height to 45m (approx. 150ft), spread to 9m (28ft). The Noble fir makes an attractive specimen, particularly when it is young. It is sometimes used as a Christmas tree and holds its needles well.

■ ABOVE
CALOCEDRUS DECURRENS (SYN. *LIBOCEDRUS DECURRENS*) (INCENSE CEDAR)

Large conifer from the western USA. In European gardens, it forms a tall, elegant spire. (Specimens in the wild are often more spreading, the habit influenced by climatic differences.) The scale-like leaves are glossy dark green. The maroon bark is fissured and flakes off; the cones are yellowish brown ageing to red-brown. Height to 30m (approx. 100ft) or more, spread to 6m (20ft) or more. The Incense cedar is magnificent as a specimen; it is resistant to honey fungus.

■ ABOVE
CEDRUS ATLANTICA 'AUREA'

Large conifer, a selection of a species (the Atlas cedar) from the Atlas Mountains in North Africa. It develops as a cone-shaped tree. The needle-like leaves, arranged in clusters, are bright golden yellow when young, then turn green; the cones are green, turning light brown. Height 40m (approx. 130ft), spread 10m (33ft). *Cedrus atlantica* 'Aurea' is slow growing and tolerates chalky soil.

■ ABOVE

CEDRUS ATLANTICA F. *GLAUCA* (BLUE ATLAS CEDAR)

Large conifer from the Atlas Mountains in North Africa. Initially cone-shaped, it develops a more spreading crown with age. The needle-like leaves, white when young but becoming bright glaucous blue, are arranged in clusters; the cones are light green. Height to 50m (164ft), spread to 10m (33ft). The Blue Atlas cedar tolerates chalky soil; it is now sometimes included within *C. libani*, as *C.l.* ssp. *atlantica* Glauca Group. (The group designation indicates that plants in cultivation may vary.)

■ ABOVE

CRYPTOMERIA JAPONICA 'ELEGANS'

Large conifer, a sterile selection of a species (the Japanese cedar) from forested areas of Japan. It forms a broad obelisk. The wedge-shaped leaves are soft and bluish green when young, turning rich bronze in autumn. Height 20m (66ft), spread 6m (20ft). *Cryptomeria japonica* 'Elegans' is one of the most widely grown cultivars; its trunk is often attractively curved. It self-layers freely.

■ OPPOSITE

CRYPTOMERIA JAPONICA 'LOBBII'

Large conifer, a selection of a species from Japan. It forms a tall, slender, conical tree. The needle-like leaves are arranged in spirals. On mature specimens the thick, fibrous bark peels away. The cones age brown. Height 25m (82ft) or more, spread to 6m (20ft). *Cryptomeria japonica* 'Lobbii' makes a handsome specimen in a large garden.

■ RIGHT

x *CUPRESSOCYPARIS LEYLANDII* 'GOLCONDA'

Large conifer, a selection of a garden hybrid (the Leyland cypress) of *Chamaecyparis nootkatensis* and *Cupressus macrocarpa*. It forms a narrow cone shape. The scale-like leaves, carried in flattened sprays, are brilliant golden yellow; the cones are brown and rounded. Height to 35m (115ft), spread to 5m (16½ft). x *Cupressocyparis leylandii* 'Golconda' is one of the most decorative of the Leyland cypresses; it can be used as a specimen as well as a hedging plant.

■ BELOW

x *CUPRESSOCYPARIS LEYLANDII* 'LEIGHTON GREEN'

Large conifer, a usually sterile selection of a garden hybrid (the Leyland cypress) of *Chamaecyparis nootkatensis* and *Cupressus macrocarpa*. It develops as a tall, narrow, cone-shaped tree. The scale-like leaves are bright green. Height to 35m (115ft), spread to 5m (16½ft). Though no less suitable for hedging than other cultivars, x *Cupressocyparis leylandii* 'Leighton Green' is perhaps best as a specimen. It produces a stronger central leader than the other cultivars and thus makes a slimmer, more elegant tree.

■ ABOVE

CUPRESSUS MACROCARPA 'DONARD GOLD'

Large conifer, a selection of a species (the Monterey cypress) from Monterey Bay, California. It forms an elegant obelisk that gradually becomes conical. The fleshy, bright yellowish-green leaves are aromatic; the cones are rounded and maroon or dark brown. Height to 30m (approx. 100ft), spread to 12m (39ft). *Cupressus macrocarpa* 'Donard Gold' is quick-growing, but is less hardy than many other conifers and is unsuitable for exposed sites.

■ BELOW

METASEQUOIA GLYPTOSTROBOIDES (DAWN REDWOOD)

Large, deciduous conifer from forested valleys of central China. It forms a narrow, cone-shaped, almost columnar tree. The leaves are light green on emergence in spring, turning pink, red, then brown in autumn, the best colour being produced on mature trees. The light brown cones, produced in hot summers only, mature darker brown. Height to 40m (approx. 130ft), spread to 5m (16½ft). The Dawn redwood appreciates moist, even waterlogged soil; it can also be grown on drier soils but will be less vigorous.

■ BELOW

PICEA OMORIKA
(SERBIAN SPRUCE)

Large conifer from Bosnia and Serbia. Initially narrowly conical, it matures to a broad obelisk. The needle-like leaves are dark green, sometimes with a bluish cast; the bark cracks in squares. The cones are purple, ripening to brown. Height 20m (66ft), spread to 3m (10ft). The Serbian spruce grows both in acid and alkaline soils and is tolerant of urban pollution.

■ ABOVE

PINUS SYLVESTRIS (SCOTS PINE)

Large conifer widely distributed throughout northern Europe and east Asia. It grows as a cone shape but develops a characteristic spreading crown with age. The grey- or blue-green, twisted needle-like leaves are carried in pairs; the pale brown cones mature darker. Height to 30m (approx. 100ft), spread to 9m (28ft). The Scots pine is exceptionally hardy and is effective planted in stands in exposed sites.

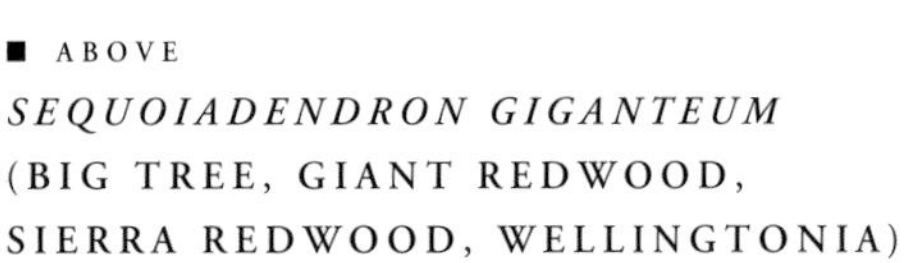

■ ABOVE

SEQUOIADENDRON GIGANTEUM (BIG TREE, GIANT REDWOOD, SIERRA REDWOOD, WELLINGTONIA)

Large conifer from California, USA. It forms a cone shape, more spreading with age; the lower branches sweep down then curve upwards. The scale-like leaves, arranged spirally, are awl-shaped, suffused with grey, and are aromatic when crushed; the cones, seldom produced on young trees, mature to pale brown. The bark is thick and fissured. Height to 80m (approx. 260ft) or more, spread to 10m (33ft). The Giant redwood is a magnificent specimen tree where space permits; it can achieve a great age.

■ ABOVE

TAXODIUM DISTICHUM (SWAMP CYPRESS)

Large, deciduous, dioecious conifer which is found in swampy ground in the south-east USA. It forms a tall cone shape that becomes untidy as it matures. The flattened needle-like leaves redden in autumn and are carried in two ranks. Purple male cones hang down and are a feature in winter; the female cones are inconspicuous. When it is grown near water, it produces special breathing roots or "knees" (known botanically as pneumatophores). Height to 40m (approx. 130ft), spread to 9m (28ft). The Swamp cypress requires wet, preferably acid soil; mature specimens have the best autumn colour, which can be brilliant.

■ ABOVE AND RIGHT

THUJA PLICATA (WESTERN RED CEDAR)

Large conifer from western North America that forms a cone-shaped tree, broadening at the crown with age. The scale-like leaves, aromatic when crushed, are carried in two ranks on stems that hang downwards at their tips. The green cones mature to brown. Height to 35m (115ft), spread to 9m (30ft) or more. Where the stems of the Western red cedar trail on the ground, they can self-layer. It is suitable for planting as a hedge.

Medium-sized conifers

■ RIGHT

ABIES DELAVAYI VAR. *FORRESTII* (*SYN. A. FORRESTII*) (FORREST FIR)

Medium-sized to large conifer from the Yunnan, China. It forms a narrow cone-shaped tree. The needle-like leaves, carried in a comb-like arrangement on the stems, are dark green above and silvery-white beneath (see inset); the cones are violet-blue. Height 10–20m (30–70ft), spread 3–6m (10–20ft). The Forrest fir, named after the famous plant-hunter George Forrest, makes rapid growth in conditions that suit it; though generally hardy, it can be unreliable in areas where prolonged cold spells are likely.

■ LEFT

CHAMAECYPARIS PISIFERA 'FILIFERA AUREA'

Medium-sized conifer (on the left), a selection of a larger species (the Sawara cypress) from southern Japan. It forms a broadly cone-shaped tree. The scale-like leaves are carried on whippy shoots that hang down; the cones age to dark brown. Height 12m (40ft), spread 5m (16½ft). *Chamaecyparis pisifera* 'Filifera Aurea' is slow-growing and is a good choice for a small to medium garden.

■ ABOVE

CUPRESSUS ARIZONICA VAR. *GLABRA* (SYN. *C. GLABRA*) (SMOOTH CYPRESS)

Medium-sized conifer from the south-west USA that forms a regular cone-shaped tree. On young specimens, the bark is smooth, reddish-purple and flaking; it thickens and turns to greyish brown on older trees. The scale-like leaves are glaucous bluish-grey and are aromatic; the cones are dark brown. Height to 15m (approx. 50ft), spread to 5m (16½ft). The Smooth cypress is a good specimen where space is limited; it succeeds in both alkaline and acid soils.

■ ABOVE

JUNIPERUS CHINENSIS 'AUREA'

Medium-sized conifer, a male selection of a larger species (the Chinese juniper) from China, Mongolia and Japan. It forms a narrow obelisk. The aromatic, dull golden-yellow leaves are wedge-shaped initially, becoming scale-like. Many cones are produced in spring. Height to 20m (66ft), spread to 6m (20ft). *Juniperus chinensis* 'Aurea' is slow-growing; it colours best in full sun and tolerates dry and chalky soils.

■ RIGHT

JUNIPERUS X *MEDIA* 'PFITZERIANA GLAUCA' (SYN. *J.* X *PFITZERIANA* 'GLAUCA')

Medium-sized conifer, a selection of a hybrid probably between *J. sabina* and *J. chinensis.* (The hybrid is thought to occur wild in Inner Mongolia.) It forms a spreading, flat-topped bush. The scale-like leaves are glaucous blue to silver. The "berries" (modified cones) are dark purple initially, developing a paler bloom as they ripen. Height 4m (13ft), spread 6m (20ft). *Juniperus* x *media* 'Pfitzeriana Glauca' is best if given space to develop its natural habit.

■ LEFT

SEQUOIA SEMPERVIRENS 'ADPRESSA'

Medium-sized conifer, a selection of a species (the Coastal redwood) from coastal California and Oregon that grows to colossal proportions. It develops a broadly conical habit, with horizontal upper branches and lower ones that sweep down to the ground. The leaves are scale-like and flattened; creamy white at first, they age to grey-green. The cones are mid-green and leathery. Height to 9m (30ft) or more, spread to 6m (20ft). *Sequoia sempervirens* 'Adpressa' is slow-growing and may exceed the dimensions given here; it is best in a damp climate.

■ BELOW

TAXUS BACCATA (YEW)

Medium-sized, dioecious conifer from Europe and North Africa to parts of the Middle East. It forms a broad, spreading, cone shape with dense horizontal branches. The needle-like leaves are glossy dark green and are carried in two ranks. Red "berries" (modified cones), each containing a single seed, are produced in autumn on female plants. Height to 20m (66ft), spread to 10m (33ft). The selection 'Lutea' (syn. *T.b.* 'Fructu-luteo') has yellow berries (see inset). The yew is a long-lived conifer; it responds well to clipping, making it ideal for hedging or topiary.

■ ABOVE

TAXUS BACCATA 'FASTIGIATA' (IRISH YEW)

Medium-sized conifer, a female selection from Florence Court in Ireland. It forms an obelisk, pointed at the crown, but spreading with age. The dark green, needle-like leaves are arranged radially on strongly upright stems; the "berries" ripen to red in autumn. Height to 10m (33ft), spread to 6m (20ft). Owing to its longevity and sombre presence, the Irish yew is widely grown in European churchyards. It can be kept within bounds by pruning and can also be wired into a narrower, more formal shape.

Small and dwarf conifers

■ ABOVE
ABIES AMABILIS 'SPREADING STAR'

Small conifer, a low-growing selection of a much larger species from mountainous regions of North America. The horizontal, spreading branches have needle-like leaves that are glossy dark green above and white beneath; they smell of oranges when crushed. The cones are deep purple. Height 50cm (20in), spread to 5m (16½ft). *Abies amabilis* 'Spreading Star' is good for ground cover; it prefers acid soil that does not dry out in summer.

■ ABOVE
ABIES BALSAMEA 'NANA'

Dwarf conifer, a selection of a much larger species (the Balsam fir) from the USA. It forms a dome-shaped bush. The aromatic, dark green, needle-like leaves, shorter than on the species, are arranged in two ranks on the stems; the cones are purplish blue. Height and spread 1m (3ft). *Abies balsamea* 'Nana' is suitable for a rock garden and tolerates some shade; it is exceptionally hardy.

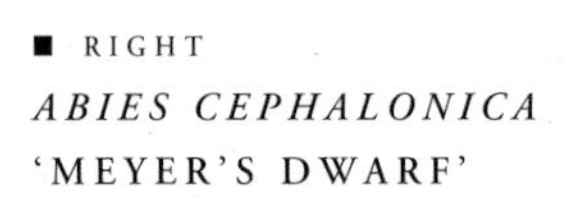

■ RIGHT
ABIES CEPHALONICA
'MEYER'S DWARF'

Dwarf conifer, a spreading selection of a much larger, upright-growing species (the Greek fir) from Greece. It forms a spreading, flat-topped mound. The needle-like leaves are glossy deep green and are shorter than on the species; the cones are greenish brown and resinous. Height 50cm (20in), spread 1.5m (5ft). *Abies cephalonica* 'Meyer's Dwarf' is good in a rock garden and tolerates some shade.

■ ABOVE

CEDRUS ATLANTICA

'GLAUCA PENDULA'

Variable conifer, a selection of a species (the Atlas cedar) from the Atlas Mountains in North Africa. It has an arching leader and develops as a tent-like structure. The needle-like leaves are glaucous blue-green; the dull green cones mature brown. Height and spread to 15m (approx. 50ft), more or less. *Cedrus atlantica* 'Glauca Pendula' is slow-growing. A dramatic specimen, it can grow taller than stated here if the central leader is strong; if the leader is removed, the horizontal branches spread wider and may need some support.

■ RIGHT

CEDRUS DEODARA

'GOLDEN HORIZON'

Usually small conifer, a selection of a much larger species (the Deodar cedar) from mountainous and forested areas from western Nepal to Afghanistan. It forms a broad cone shape. The horizontal branches hang down at their tips. The young, needle-like leaves are bright yellow; the female cones are glaucous blue, maturing to brown. Height 5m (16½ft), spread 2.5m (8ft), but sometimes bigger. *Cedrus deodara* 'Golden Horizon' is a vigorous conifer that tolerates chalky soil; if it is grown in shade, the leaves are bluish green.

■ BELOW

CHAMAECYPARIS LAWSONIANA 'AUREA DENSA'

Small or dwarf conifer, a selection of a much larger species (the Lawson cypress) from western North America. It forms a rounded shrub. The bright golden-yellow leaves are needle-like initially, becoming scale-like; the cones are glaucous or rust-brown. Height and spread to 1.2m (4ft). 'Aurea Densa' is one of the outstanding golden-leaved cultivars of *Chamaecyparis lawsoniana.*

■ ABOVE

CHAMAECYPARIS LAWSONIANA 'BLEU NANTAIS'

Dwarf conifer, a usually sterile selection of a much larger species (the Lawson cypress) from western North America. It forms a rounded cone shape. The juvenile foliage is needle-like, becoming scale-like, and is bright glaucous blue. Height and spread 1.5m (5ft). *Chamaecyparis lawsoniana* 'Bleu Nantais' is a good choice for a rock garden.

■ OPPOSITE ABOVE LEFT

CHAMAECYPARIS OBTUSA 'NANA GRACILIS'

Small or dwarf conifer, a selection of a larger species (the Hinoki cypress) from southern Japan. It forms a rough pyramid. The leaves are scale-like and bright glossy green; the cones age from green to brown. Height 2m (6½ft) or more, spread to 2m (6½ft). *Chamaecyparis obtusa* 'Nana Gracilis' is less tolerant of lime than other members of the genus; it is a good choice for a rock garden.

■ LEFT

JUNIPERUS COMMUNIS 'HIBERNICA'

Small conifer, a selection of a larger species (the Common juniper) found throughout the northern hemisphere. It forms a narrow, upright obelisk. The needle-like leaves have a bluish green cast; the "berries", initially green, ripen to black over three years. Height 3–5m (10–16½ft), spread 30cm (1ft). Tolerant of chalky soils, *Juniperus communis* 'Hibernica' is sometimes referred to as the "Irish" juniper.

■ RIGHT

JUNIPERUS HORIZONTALIS (CREEPING JUNIPER)

Spreading conifer from North America. It forms a mat of greyish-green leaves that are needle-like when young, becoming scale-like. The "berries" are dark blue. Height to 30cm (1ft), spread to 2m (6½ft) or more. *Juniperus horizontalis* has many attractive cultivars, all suitable for ground cover. 'Blue Moon' is glaucous blue, 'Douglasii' is bluish green, turning rich purple in autumn, and 'Golden Carpet' is bright yellowish green.

■ ABOVE

JUNIPERUS **X** *MEDIA* 'SULPHUR SPRAY'

Dwarf conifer, a selection of a hybrid between probably *J. sabina* and *J. chinensis.* (The hybrid is thought to occur wild in Inner Mongolia.) It forms a spreading, flat-topped bush that can be table-like on maturity. The scale-like leaves are bright yellowish green; the "berries" are dark purple initially but develop a bluish bloom as they ripen. Height 1m (3ft), spread 2m (6½ft). 'Sulphur Spray' is one of several cultivars grouped under *Juniperus* x *media* that are more or less indistinguishable from one another; others include the widely grown 'Pfitzeriana Aurea'.

■ LEFT

PICEA GLAUCA 'ECHINIFORMIS'

Dwarf conifer, a selection of a much larger species (the White spruce) from northern Europe. It forms a rounded cone shape. The needle-like leaves are blue-grey. The light green cones mature to brown. Height 1.5m (5ft), spread 1m (3ft). *Picea glauca* 'Echiniformis' makes an attractive specimen in a small garden and is also good in containers.

■ ABOVE

PICEA ABIES 'GREGORYANA'

Dwarf conifer, a selection of a much larger species (the Norway spruce) from southern Scandinavia to central and southern Europe. It produces a virtually impenetrable mound of dark green, needle-like leaves; the cones age from dark green to brown. Height and spread 60cm (2ft). Slow growing, *Picea abies* 'Gregoryana' is one of the most compact of all the dwarf conifers.

■ RIGHT

PICEA GLAUCA VAR. *ALBERTIANA* 'ALBERTA GLOBE'

Small or dwarf conifer, a mutation of the selection 'Conica'; the species is found in North America. It forms a dome shape. The needle-like leaves are blue green; cones may not appear. Height and spread 1m (3ft). *Picea glauca* var. *albertiana* 'Alberta Globe' is a good choice for a rock garden.

■ ABOVE

PICEA PUNGENS 'GLOBOSA'

Dwarf conifer, a selection of a much larger species (the Colorado spruce) from the USA. It forms a domed or mound-shaped plant. The slightly glaucous green leaves are bristle-like and arranged radially; the cones age from green to light brown. Height and spread 1m (3ft). *Picea pungens* 'Globosa' is one of many dwarf forms of the species, all making excellent garden plants.

■ ABOVE

PICEA GLAUCA VAR. *ALBERTIANA* 'CONICA'

Small or dwarf conifer. The species is found in North America; the variant *albertiana*, of which this is a selection, occurs in the Canadian Rocky Mountains. It forms a dense cone shape. The blue-green, needle-like leaves are permanently juvenile; cones may not appear. Height to 4m (13ft), spread 2m (6½ft). *Picea glauca* var. *albertiana* 'Conica' is a neat-growing conifer.

■ RIGHT

PICEA PUNGENS 'MONTGOMERY'

Dwarf conifer, a selection of a much larger species (the Colorado spruce) from the USA. It forms a broad-based, cone-shaped plant. The silvery blue leaves are bristle-like and arranged radially; the cones age from green to light brown. Height 1.5m (5ft), spread 1m (3ft). Slow-growing, *Picea pungens* 'Montgomery' would be among the first choices for a specimen in a small garden.

■ ABOVE AND INSET

PINUS MUGO 'CORLEY'S MAT'

Dwarf conifer, a selection of a species (the Dwarf mountain pine) from central Europe. It forms a prostrate, spreading mat. The long, needle-like, bright green leaves are well spaced on very resinous stems; the cones are dark brown. Height 1m (3ft), spread 2m (6½ft). *Pinus mugo* 'Corley's Mat' is good in a rock garden.

■ RIGHT

PLATYCLADUS ORIENTALIS 'AURESCENS' (SYN. *THUJA ORIENTALIS* 'AUREA NANA')

Dwarf conifer, a selection of a much larger species from China and Iran. It makes an egg-shaped plant. The scale-like leaves are aromatic, yellowish-green and tinged bronze in autumn; they are held in irregular, vertical, fan-like plates. The cones are flagon-like and bluish-green, maturing to grey. Height and spread to 60cm (2ft). *Platycladus orientalis* 'Aurescens' is an outstanding conifer for a small garden.

■ ABOVE

PLATYCLADUS ORIENTALIS 'SIEBOLDII' (SYN. *THUJA ORIENTALIS* 'SIEBOLDII')

Small conifer, a selection of a much larger species from China and Iran. It makes an egg-shaped plant. The aromatic, scale-like, mid-green leaves are carried in stiff, vertical plates. Height to 3m (10ft), spread to 1.8m (6ft). *Platycladus orientalis* 'Sieboldii' is a good dwarf for combining with heathers or other low-growing conifers.

■ ABOVE

TAXUS BACCATA 'FASTIGIATA AUREOMARGINATA'

Small or medium-sized conifer, a further variant of a female selection (*T. b.* 'Fastigiata', the Irish yew) of a larger species (the yew) from Europe and North Africa to Iran. It forms a broad obelisk. The dark green, needle-like leaves have bright yellow margins and are radially arranged on strongly vertical branches. The "berries" ripen to red in autumn. Height to 5m (16½ft), spread to 2.5m (8ft). *Taxus baccata* 'Fastigiata Aureomarginata' makes a smaller but proportionately broader plant than its parent.

■ LEFT

TAXUS BACCATA 'REPANDENS'

Small or dwarf conifer, a female selection of a species (the yew) from Europe and North Africa to Iran. It does not produce a strong vertical leader but forms a mat of spreading branches near ground level. The leaves are dark green. Red "berries" (modified cones), each containing a single seed, are produced in autumn. Height to 60cm (2ft), spread to 5m (16½ft). *Taxus baccata* 'Repandens' makes good ground cover; it is best without extensive pruning that might affect its natural spreading habit.

■ ABOVE

TAXUS BACCATA 'STANDISHII'

Small or dwarf conifer, a female selection of a larger species (the yew) from Europe, North Africa and Iran. It forms a slim column. The bright yellowish green, needle-like leaves are radially arranged on strongly upright stems. The "berries" ripen to red in autumn. Height 1.5m (5ft), spread 60cm (2ft). *Taxus baccata* 'Standishii' is one of the most decorative of the yews and is an excellent choice for a small garden.

■ ABOVE

THUJA OCCIDENTALIS 'ERICOIDES'

Dwarf conifer, a selection of a much larger species from eastern North America. It forms a broad, sometimes rounded obelisk. The spreading, juvenile, scale-like leaves are green in summer, turning rich brown in autumn; they are aromatic when crushed. The cones age from yellow to brown. Height and spread 1.2m (4ft). *Thuja occidentalis* 'Ericoides' appreciates moist soil and is best with some protection from hot sun and cold, drying winds.

■ ABOVE

THUJA PLICATA 'IRISH GOLD'

Usually dwarf conifer, a selection of a much larger species from North America. It forms a conical shrub. The scale-like leaves are bright yellow-green with lighter patches; the cones are green initially, maturing to brown. Height and spread generally to 2m (6½ft), though it can eventually reach a height of 20m (66ft) or more. 'Irish Gold' is one of the most decorative selections of *Thuja plicata.*

Buying a conifer

Conifers are sold as container-grown or root-balled plants, and only occasionally (unlike deciduous trees) as bare-root plants. Container-grown plants, generally available year-round at garden centres, are young plants that have been raised in containers, and are seldom taller than 90cm (3ft). Root-balled plants are often more mature and can be as high as 1.2m (4ft) or more. They are grown in rows in open fields and are lifted for sale in the autumn or early spring. The soil ball is wrapped in permeable material to prevent desiccation, or is held in place in a wire cage or net. Root-balled conifers are available at conifer nurseries and can sometimes be found at garden centres.

When buying root-balled plants, if possible go to a local nursery where the climate and soil conditions are similar to those in your own garden. Conifers are vulnerable to transplant shock (see Transplanting an established conifer), and it is advisable to minimize this as far as is possible. Check whether the plant was grown at the nursery: it may have been grown elsewhere and bought in. You may be able to select your conifer from those in the field, and it may be lifted fresh then and there. If you are looking for a particular cultivar or an unusual species, you may have to buy a conifer that has been imported from a nursery outside your area.

Generally, only deciduous conifers and Christmas trees are available bare-root (lifted from the ground and their roots shaken free of soil), usually in the autumn.

Container-grown plants can be planted at any time of the year, except when the ground is waterlogged or frozen or during periods of prolonged drought. Root-balled conifers should be planted in

■ BELOW
A root-balled yew. The soil ball is held together by a net and strong elastic bands.

■ BELOW
Deciduous conifers such as larch are sometimes sold as bare-root plants.

the autumn or early spring, as soon after purchase as possible. If it is not possible to plant a root-balled conifer straight away, owing to adverse conditions, keep the tree in a cool, shaded, frost-free place and cover the rootball with garden soil or hessian (sacking) to stop the roots drying out.

When buying a conifer of either type, look for a specimen that is growing evenly with no sign of any damage, bearing in mind that most conifers do not regenerate freely from damaged wood (see Pruning). Any bare patches on the stem are likely to remain bare. Also avoid plants that have two or more leaders (the main stem of a plant) and any plants that have large brown patches. Where practical, slide container-grown conifers out of their pots and inspect the rootball. If the compost (soil mix) falls away, the plant does not have a sufficiently good root system. If the roots are tightly coiled around the pot, it is rootbound and will be slow to establish – indeed, it may not establish at all. When buying root-balled conifers, always carry them by supporting them underneath the root-ball, and not by the stem. Otherwise the soil may begin to fall away, exposing the roots to the light and possibly damaging them.

Garden centres normally sell conifers, such as this spruce, as container-grown plants.

It is essential to check the eventual height of the conifer before making a purchase. Different cultivars of the same species can have radically different heights and it is difficult, if not impossible, to tell the difference when confronted by two young plants in the garden centre. Furthermore, many conifers sold as dwarfs are better described as slow-growing. While they may persist as small plants for a number of years, eventually they may become huge trees outgrowing the small space they were allotted. They may still be the appropriate choice if you bear in mind that you may have to dig them up later and either discard them or move them elsewhere (see Transplanting an established conifer). There are many conifers, however, that are true dwarfs that seldom exceed 2m (6½ft) in height.

Planting

Choose the planting site with care, particularly for large conifers, which may fail in adverse conditions. Most need an open site, but certain situations are undesirable. A position in a frost pocket (at the foot of a slope, for instance) will lead to potential damage, since cold air will collect there. Remember also that cold, drying winds in winter, even if the temperature is above freezing, can be as detrimental as hard frosts, so choose a site that is sheltered initially. If you live near the coast, limit yourself to varieties of conifer that are tolerant of salt sprays.

You should also avoid planting in a site that is likely to be excessively dry – near a wall, for example. Remember that conifers that eventually reach a great height will have comparably large root systems that not only take moisture out of the soil but may also damage nearby house foundations and drains. Large conifers should be planted at least 10m (33ft) away from any masonry, preferably more.

Most soil types are suitable, but very alkaline soil will not support all genera. The ideal is a fairly heavy, fertile, moist but well-drained loam (consisting of roughly equal parts of sand, silt, clay and decayed organic

PLANTING A CONIFER

1 Prepare the site by digging over the ground, removing all perennial weeds and forking in organic matter.

2 Dig a hole of the appropriate size and fork in a handful of bonemeal at the base to promote root growth.

3 Set the conifer (here root-balled) in position in the middle of the hole and check the planting depth. The soil mark on the plant should be at the same level as the surrounding soil. If the conifer is container-grown, check that the compost surface is level with the surrounding soil.

4 Remove the wrapping around the soil ball, rocking the conifer from side to side if necessary. If planting a container-grown conifer slide it out of its pot and tease out as many of the roots as possible with a hand fork. Backfill with the excavated soil.

5 Firm the soil with your foot, but do not compact the surface. This could lead to "capping", where the soil surface forms a crust that prevents the free passage of air and water through the roots.

6 Water in well, then apply a mulch at least 5cm (2in) deep over the planting area to prevent evaporation from the soil surface. Keep wet mulches well away from the stem: contact could lead to rotting.

matter). Only cypresses, junipers and pines thrive on poor, sandy soils. *Metasequoia* and *Taxodium* need wet, even swampy, soil. All soils are improved by digging in organic matter, either well-rotted farmyard manure or garden compost, before planting. This improves the drainage on heavy soils and holds moisture and nutrients on dry soils.

Timing of planting depends on whether you are planting a container-grown or root-balled plant (see Buying a conifer). Autumn planting is generally successful, since the conifer's roots will grow away into the still-warm soil and establish before fresh top-growth is initiated the following spring. However, in very cold areas subject to heavy frosts, delay planting until spring.

Dig a large hole, at least two or three times the width of the container or rootball and twice the depth. If the conifer is a large one, a hole of about 1m (3ft) across is appropriate. If you are planting in grass, remove the turf first, but do not replace it after planting, since it will rob the conifer of available moisture.

Keep conifers well watered during the first two or three years after planting and mist during periods of drought (in the evening on hot days) to prevent the foliage drying out. Feed annually with a general-purpose fertilizer, applied according to the manufacturer's instructions. A handful of bonemeal forked around the base in autumn is beneficial to root growth. Mulch well in spring or autumn to conserve moisture in the soil. Once established conifers do not need regular feeding and watering.

Conifers that tolerate coastal sites
Chamaecyparis
x *Cupressocyparis leylandii*
Cupressus macrocarpa
Cupressus sempervirens
Juniperus
Pinus contorta (coastal strains)
Pinus nigra var. *nigra*
Pinus radiata
Pinus sylvestris

Conifers for alkaline soil
Cedrus
Chamaecyparis
x *Cupressocyparis*
Cupressus
Juniperus
Picea (some)
Pinus (some)
Taxus

Growing conifers in containers

All small and dwarf conifers are suitable for growing in containers. Slow-growing species and cultivars are particularly recommended. They can stay in the same container for several years without needing repotting, keeping root disturbance to a minimum. You could group them together in containers of different sizes, or plant several dwarf varieties together in a large sink or trough. Alternatively, use pairs to frame a doorway, or one alone to mark a focal point. Small topiary specimens are particularly effective for this purpose (see Pruning). Pines and junipers are

PLANTING A CONIFER IN A CONTAINER

1 Line the base of the container with stones, gravel or crocks to improve drainage and provide stability. Conifers in containers can become top-heavy and blow over in strong winds.

2 Begin to fill with loam-based compost (soil mix). For improved drainage, use three parts compost to one of horticultural grit or sharp sand, or replace up to half the mixture with garden compost.

3 Set the conifer in the middle of the container and check the planting depth. You should leave a gap of about 2.5cm (1in) between the top of the compost and the rim of the container.

4 Slide the conifer from its pot and gently tease out some of the roots with a hand fork.

5 Place the conifer in the middle of the container and backfill with more compost (soil mix).

6 Water well and top-dress with horticultural grit to prevent excessive water evaporation from the surface.

■ RIGHT
A conifer in a container can be moved around the garden at will.

likely to be the most successful if you have an exposed site. *Pinus mugo* is a good choice because it has an interesting shape even before it matures. Prostrate conifers, such as *Juniperus sabina* 'Tamariscifolia', are also effective in containers.

Container-grown conifers that have been grown in a sterilized, proprietary compost (soil mix) are more likely to succeed in a pot or trough than conifers bought as root-balled plants (see Buying a conifer). The latter will have been grown on in the open ground, and their soil balls will contain soil organisms that may become a problem in a container.

Choose a container about 5cm (2in) wider and deeper than the one the conifer was bought in, allowing for more root growth. Larger-growing conifers should be potted on into bigger containers every one or two years. When they eventually grow too large for a container, plant them out in the garden.

Conifers are heavy plants that can easily blow over in strong winds unless given good ballast. For maximum stability use terracotta, stone or concrete containers.

For the best results, plant the conifers in a heavy, nutrient-high, loam-based compost (soil mix). Incorporate some horticultural grit in the lowest layer of compost (soil mix) to improve drainage and add extra weight to the container. Top-dress with grit to prevent moisture loss.

Conifers grown in containers are subject to the same problems as plants in the open ground (see Conifer problems), but they need more care and attention particularly regarding watering and feeding, especially in summer. Feed during the growing season with a general-purpose fertilizer applied at the rate recommended by the manufacturer. Water the plants regularly to prevent the compost (soil mix) from drying out. On hot, dry days, mist the foliage in the evening to prevent needle-drop (see Conifer problems).

Transplanting an established conifer

Since conifers are very susceptible to transplant shock, move them only if it is essential – for instance if they have outgrown their allotted space, or are failing to thrive in their original position. Take extreme care in order to minimize disturbance to the plant. Adequate preparation of the new site and good aftercare are also essential for success.

Nevertheless, provided you follow the guidelines given below, you will stand an excellent chance of moving even quite large, established conifers successfully. The younger the plant the quicker it will re-establish.

Conifers are heavy trees. Moving even relatively small specimens may well require two people. For large specimens earth-moving equipment may be necessary, both to prepare the site and to move the conifer.

MOVING A CONIFER

1 Prepare the new site. Dig a hole about 1m (3ft) across and 60cm (2ft) deep, and loosen the soil at the base.

2 Fork organic matter and a handful of bonemeal into the hole. Tie in the branches to make it easier to handle.

3 Dig a trench around the conifer, of the same circumference as the lowest branches, if possible.

4 Fork away some of the soil from the edge of the root system, leaving a central ball of soil intact.

5 Cut through any thick, intractable roots with secateurs.

6 With a stabbing action, cut through the underside of the rootball with a spade to sever any downward-growing roots.

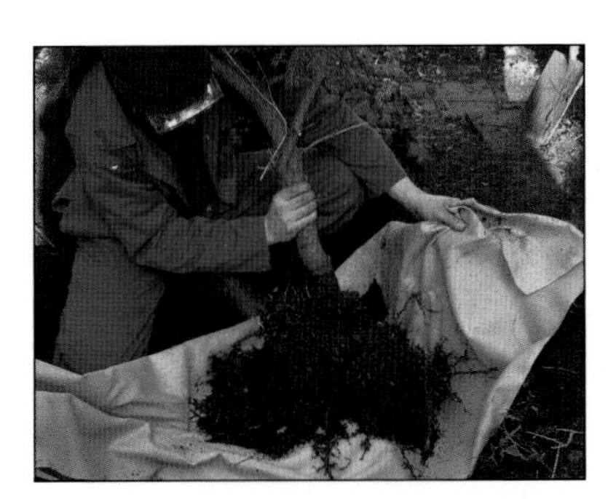

7 Rock the conifer from side to side and work a piece of hessian (sacking) or other strong material around the rootball.

8 Tie the hessian (sacking) securely around the base of the trunk.

9 Move the conifer to its new position, holding it underneath the rootball, not by the stem.

10 Remove the material and check the planting depth. You should plant the conifer at the same level in the ground as before, so check the soil mark at the base of the stem (see inset).

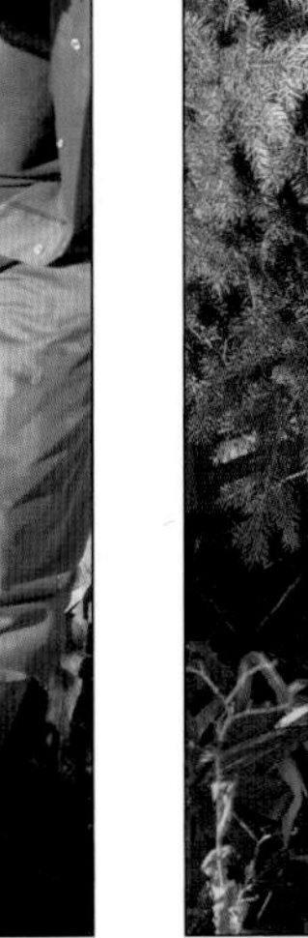

11 Backfill with the excavated soil, then firm in and water well.

12 Mulch well to conserve moisture in the soil.

To avoid injury, such operations are probably best left to professional arboriculturalists.

Transplanting is best carried out in early to mid-autumn, when the top-growth has ceased, but while the roots are still active. Choose a mild day, ideally after rainfall, when the conifer is least likely to lose excessive moisture.

Some damage to the root system is unavoidable and to an extent is desirable. It will stimulate the formation of fresh, fibrous, feeding roots that will readily take up moisture from the soil, helping the plant to re-establish itself.

Always wear goggles when you are dealing with large plants; conifer needles are sharp and could cause a serious eye injury.

Conifer hedges

Certain conifers make splendid subjects for hedges: they are evergreen and dense-growing.

The classic choice is yew, which, with its dense, dark green foliage, is the ideal foil for many garden plants. Given good cultivation yew can grow 30cm (1ft) a season and reach a height of 2m (6½ft) in five to seven years. *Thuja* makes a less dense hedge than yew or Leyland cypress (x *Cupressocyparis leylandii*) but has the advantage of aromatic leaves.

In a large, open garden, choose a quick-growing conifer for a windbreak – the Leyland cypress is ideal. Grow with minimum clipping to make a tall, feathery hedge.

You can mix plants for a "tapestry" effect. Different cultivars of Leyland cypress have different colours, for instance 'Castlewellan' has bright green foliage tipped with gold, while 'Harlequin' has patches of ivory white. You can also mix genera: interplant yew with holly or box, for instance.

Buying hedging

Hedging conifers are usually inexpensive and are often even cheaper if bought in quantity. They can be found in nurseries, garden centres, DIY stores and occasionally in supermarkets. If you need to buy in quantity (say in hundreds), you will probably get the best deal from a nursery specializing in hedging. For large quantities, most garden centres usually need to order in advance.

Hedging conifers are sold in containers, as root-balled plants or as bare-root plants, and are usually

Regularly trimmed, yew makes a hedge with a dense, even surface.

Leyland cypress makes a quick-growing hedge with a feathery surface.

■ OPPOSITE TOP
Conifers interplanted with deciduous trees make a highly effective windbreak.

available in a range of sizes. Bare-root plants 30cm (1ft) tall or less are best. To calculate the number of plants needed, divide the length of the hedge by the planting distance recommended in the table.

■ LEFT
Leyland cypresses and other hedging conifers are available in a range of sizes.

CONIFERS SUITABLE FOR HEDGING
Recommended planting distances are in parentheses.
Chamaecyparis lawsoniana (90cm/3ft)
x *Cupressocyparis leylandii* (75cm/30in)
Taxus baccata (45cm/18in)
Thuja plicata (45cm/18in)
Tsuga heterophylla (45–60cm/18–24in)

Planting a hedge

Prepare the ground as for planting a single conifer (see Planting), then dig a trench 30–90cm (1–3ft) across, depending on the size of the plants, and 20–30cm (8–12in) deep. Fork in bonemeal at the base of the trench. Space the plants according to the recommendations in the table. (Do not set small plants closer than the recommended spacing.) For a denser hedge, plant two rows, staggering the plants in a zigzag with 38cm (15in) between the rows. Backfill with the excavated soil, water well, and mulch.

Feed and water the hedge until established. On newly planted hedges clip back any straggly side branches but leave the leaders unpruned until they have reached the required height. For details on pruning an established hedge, see Pruning.

■ BOTTOM
Field grown hedging conifers are often lifted and then heeled in in rows before being put on sale.

Pruning

Conifers do not need extensive pruning, and most are best if allowed to achieve their natural shape. Occasionally, however, pruning is required, usually to repair damage, or to remove wayward or uncharacteristic growth, such as green patches on a yellow conifer.

Conifers that have a strong vertical habit display a characteristic known as central leader dominance. A single stem, ending in a terminal bud, grows upwards, thickening to form a solid trunk. The stems that arise from this (the laterals) grow horizontally. Sometimes, usually as a result of damage, two leaders develop. It is vital to remove one or the tree will not develop its characteristic shape and the fork in the trunk will be a weak point that is prone to further damage. If the leader itself is damaged, cut it below the break and attach a cane to it. Bend a strong-growing, suitably placed lateral upwards and tie it to the cane. This will then assume the characteristics of the leader. Any damage that occurs to large specimens is best treated by a qualified tree surgeon.

Where there are patches of dead foliage, cut these out completely and tie in the surrounding laterals to cover the gap. Only yew and *Cryptomeria* respond well to hard pruning.

Most conifers produce resinous sap that bleeds freely from the stems if they are cut while the tree is in active growth. Pruning is therefore best carried out from autumn to mid-winter while the tree is dormant. Use sharp, clean pruning tools – blunt blades will snag the wood, providing an entry point for disease. Wear gloves and goggles and, if you are using power machinery, the protective clothing recommended.

REMOVING A COMPETING LEADER

1 Where two or more leaders have formed, leave the stronger or strongest unpruned. Cut away the other stem or stems at the point of origin.

2 If the remaining leader is not growing strongly upright, as here, tie a cane to the conifer's main stem. Tie the new leader to the cane to encourage vertical growth.

REMOVING A WAYWARD SHOOT

If a conifer produces an uncharacteristic or wayward shoot, cut it back to its point of origin with secateurs or, if the branch is thick, with loppers.

■ LEFT
Conifer hedges are best shaped with an inward slope (a "batter") as a defence against heavy snowfalls.

Pruning a hedge

After planting (see Conifer hedges), allow the central leader on all hedging conifers to develop unpruned.

Once the conifers have grown about 60cm (2ft) higher than the desired final height of the hedge, cut them back to 30cm (1ft) lower than the desired height. For yew, which is slower-growing than most hedging plants, simply allow the hedge to grow to the required height after planting, then trim it.

Trim the laterals as the conifers grow so that the hedge tapers towards the top, forming a rough triangle when seen in cross-section. This will allow light to reach the lower branches, which might otherwise become bare. It also prevents snow from settling on the top of the hedge, which could cause the upper branches to splay outwards and break.

Clip over established hedges twice a year – three or four times for Leyland cypress – in late spring and late summer. To keep the top of the hedge level, run a length of string between two posts at either end of the hedge to act as a guide. If you use power machinery, wear the protective clothing recommended by the manufacturer.

Topiary

A few conifers are suitable for topiary – the art of clipping evergreens into geometric or other shapes. The best conifer for this purpose is yew, which responds well to being cut back and provides a dense, even surface. Domes and cone shapes are the easiest for the beginner. If you have a good eye, you can cut them free-hand; alternatively you can make a simple framework to guide you. With other conifers you cannot achieve the same detail but, as they form a dominant leader, it is a relatively simple matter to create a standard. Allow a plant to grow to the desired height, then cut away the unwanted foliage. Shape the head with secateurs.

A striking though seldom practised technique is that of "cloud" pruning, found illustrated on "willow-pattern" china. Only the shorter-growing forms of *Cryptomeria japonica* are suitable for this, however. Allow the plant to grow unpruned until the central leader has reached 2m (6½ft) in height, then cut this back to 60–90cm (2–3ft) to stimulate the side shoots to develop and thicken. Thereafter, the main branches should be left unpruned and further pruning should be restricted to clipping over the foliage into ball or cloud shapes.

CONIFERS SUITABLE FOR TOPIARY

- x *Cupressocyparis leylandii*
- *Cupressus arizonica* 'Fastigiata'
- *Cupressus macrocarpa*
- *Cryptomeria japonica* (some cvs.)
- *Taxus baccata*

Propagation

Conifers can be propagated by a variety of methods. The two simplest are seed and cuttings. Propagation by seed can be used for all species; named varieties can only be increased by vegetative methods. A few conifers are best increased by grafting, but this is a nurseryman's technique that is seldom practised.

Propagation by seed

In autumn gather fresh, unopened cones from the ground. To extract the seed, leave the cones in a warm, dry place until they open, then tap out the seed on to a sheet of paper. Cedar cones need to be soaked in warm water before the scales will open to release the seed. Dry the seed on absorbent kitchen paper.

Yew and juniper "berries", which are fleshy, need slightly different treatment. Squash the berries when they are ripe and rub out the seeds. Wash them clean in warm water, then dry them on kitchen paper.

Conifer seed is often slow to germinate and needs a period of cold to break its dormancy (a process known as stratification). You can sow the seed as normal and place the containers outside over winter, allowing stratification to occur naturally, or speed it up by chilling the seed before sowing. Even so, seed may take two years to germinate, especially that of Mediterranean and Mexican pines.

To stratify conifer seed artificially, mix it with moistened peat, perlite or vermiculite. Then seal the seed in a polythene bag, and place it in a freezer for about three weeks.

EXTRACTING SEED FROM CONES

Gather the cones in autumn. Tap out the seeds on to a sheet of paper, then store in a cool dark place in paper bags until you are ready to sow them.

EXTRACTING YEW OR JUNIPER SEED

1 Squash the ripe "berries" between finger and thumb to extract the seeds, and wash them in warm water. Dry the seeds on absorbent kitchen paper.

2 Mix with damp peat (or an alternative), perlite or vermiculite and seal in a polythene bag. Place the bag in a freezer for about three weeks.

SOWING THE SEED

1 Prepare pots of seed compost. Water well and allow to drain. Scatter the seed thinly, then cover it with a little compost and top with horticultural grit.

2 Place the containers outside. Pot up the seedlings when they are large enough to handle. Grow them on until they are large enough to plant out.

Cuttings

Propagation by cuttings is used to produce plants that are identical to the parent. Use cuttings material that is characteristic of the plant you wish to increase. If you take a cutting from a horizontal branch of a very upright plant, the new plant will have a spreading rather than a vertical habit.

Conifer cuttings can be taken from mid- to late summer (semi-ripe) or from late summer to early autumn (fully ripe). Fully ripe cuttings are best taken with a "heel". Grasp a stem near its base and pull it away sharply, tearing a strip of bark from the main branch. Trim the strip with a knife. Treat all cuttings with hormone rooting compound.

Prepare a cuttings compost (soil) of equal parts of peat (or alternative) and horticultural grit or sand. Insert the cuttings into pots or trays of the compost (soil) and keep them in a cold frame until rooted, usually by late spring the following year. Pot them up individually into loam-based compost (soil) and grow them on for a year or two before planting them out in their final positions. Fully ripe cuttings can also be rooted in a sheltered spot in the open ground, though the percentage of cuttings that strike is likely to be lower. In very cold weather, it may be necessary to protect the cuttings with cloches.

TAKING A FULLY RIPE CUTTING WITH A HEEL

1 **Grasp the stem close to its point of origin and pull it sharply away from the main stem, tearing away a piece of bark.**

2 **Trim the heel with a sharp knife and then follow the steps for semi-ripe cuttings illustrated below.**

PROPAGATION BY SEMI-RIPE CUTTINGS

1 **Take a cutting 10–15cm (4–6in) long from a shoot characteristic of the parent; pinch out the tip if it is very soft.**

2 **Pare a sliver of bark about 2.5cm (1in) from the base of the cutting and dip the base in hormone rooting powder.**

3 **Insert cuttings in the compost (half horticultural grit or sand and peat). Pot up the cuttings when they have rooted.**

Conifer problems

The majority of conifers are relatively trouble-free provided that they are growing strongly in conditions that suit them. They have not been subjected to intensive breeding programmes and are not as susceptible to attack by pests and diseases as some other highly bred types of plant.

Many of the problems you are likely to encounter in gardens are weather- or climate-related, though there are a few pests and diseases that can cause damage.

Weather and climate problems

Conifers are prone to weather damage at any stage of their development. In all cases, where it is feasible, it is better to take preventive rather than remedial action.

In winter young conifers are particularly susceptible to cold, drying winds that can cause dieback. Prolonged periods of drought during the summer months can be equally detrimental.

Large specimens can be damaged by heavy snowfalls. Tall specimens grown on hilltops or in other exposed situations are vulnerable to lightning strikes or can be ripped apart by strong gales. They are also a potential hazard if planted too close to buildings or thoroughfares.

In winter and early spring protect young conifers in exposed sites from both winds and heavy frosts. Insert stakes in the ground around the tree, then attach a length of horticultural fleece or tightly woven netting around it. Weight the fleece or netting down at the edges to prevent draughts, but keep the top open. It is important that any material you use is air-permeable, so that the conifer does not "sweat" and create a stagnant atmosphere. Remove the protection when the weather turns more favourable.

***Chamaecyparis* 'Ellwood's Gold' showing reversion.**

Conifers that have an upright habit, such as the Irish yew, Irish juniper and some *Chamaecyparis* cultivars, can be damaged by falls of snow that can pull down branches and even tear them from the tree. To minimize the risk, wind horticultural twine or wire around the tree to tie the branches in.

It is usually not practical to protect large trees. If a storm or heavy fall of snow causes serious harm, seek the advice of a professional tree surgeon. Old, badly wounded specimens may not recover and may have to be removed.

If you have a garden with a large tree that is protected by a preservation order, make sure you are adequately insured against any potential risk to your property or to that of neighbours and third parties; take legal advice before carrying out any work on the tree.

In summer, to minimize the risk of desiccation on newly planted conifers (except those adapted to drought, such as cypresses and junipers), spray the foliage every day in hot spells, in the evening to reduce moisture loss.

Dieback caused by a damaged stem or wind damage.

Pests and diseases

Conifers vary in their susceptibility to pests and diseases. Good cultivation generally keeps the trees in good health and growing strongly. Pines and larches are generally trouble-free. Spruces are prone to a number of problems. Pines and *Tsuga* tend to resist honey fungus. Members of Cupressaceae are vulnerable to scale insect, aphids and crown rots. *Cupressus macrocarpa is* susceptible to canker rot.

A juniper showing aphid honeydew damage.

Where the use of sprays is recommended, apply them during still, cloudy weather. Winds would disperse the spray (the conifer would not benefit and the product could harm other neighbouring plants), and hot sun could cause scorch as the solvent evaporates. When using any chemical control, always follow the manufacturer's instructions to the letter. Dilute the product as directed and wear any protective clothing recommended.

Crown rot

Vulnerable plants: Potentially all conifers.
How to identify: The conifers fail to make good growth; the lower part of the stem begins to rot and fungi may take hold.
Cause: Any fungi or bacteria that enter the plant's organism through bark wounds to the main stem.
Prevention. Take care not to damage the trunks of conifers when planting. Always plant to the correct level: deep planting brings potentially harmful soil bacteria into contact with the stem. When applying deep wet mulches, keep them clear of the trunk.
Control: Not possible.

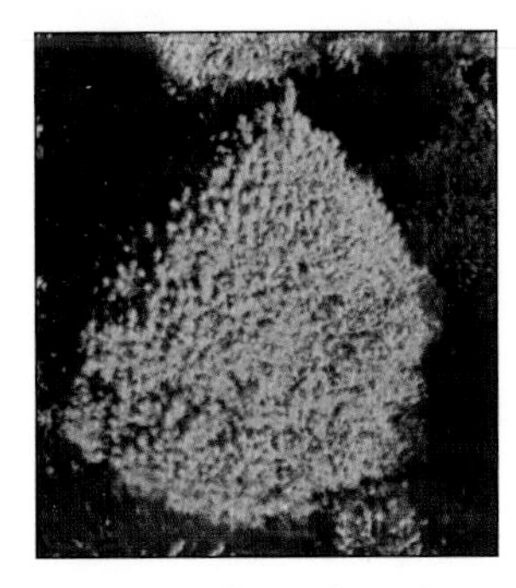

A conifer suffering from the effects of drought.

Seriously affected conifers should be dug up and burnt.

Canker rot

Vulnerable plants: Potentially all conifers.
How to identify: The stems distort: sunken patches appear on the bark followed by a swelling of the stem.

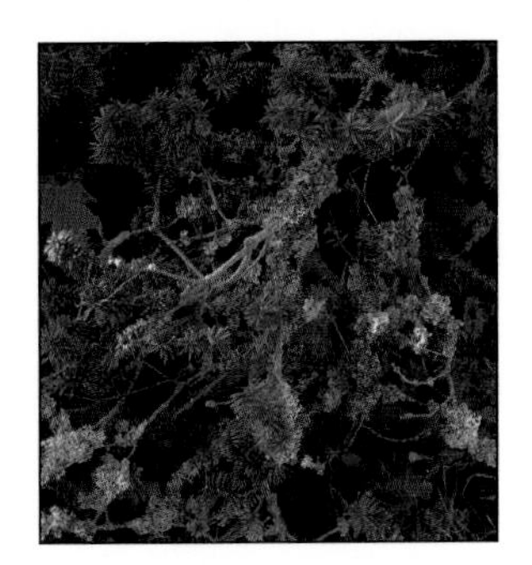

Lichen damage usually caused by damp conditions.

Cause: A number of fungi and bacteria.
Prevention: Not possible.
Control: Cut back diseased stems to healthy growth and destroy them. Spray with a general garden fungicide such as copper fungicide, repeating at monthly intervals.

Conifer spinning mite

Vulnerable plants: All conifers, particularly firs, spruces and some pines.
How to identify: The conifer leaves develop a bronze tinge and may be shed.
Cause: The conifer spinning mite (a type of red spider mite), a sap-sucking insect that is most prevalent in warm climates.
Prevention: Avoid planting conifers in humid areas.
Control: Spray with malathion or derris, repeating as recommended.

Honey fungus

Vulnerable plants: Most conifers, particularly when young; yews, *Libocedrus,* larches and *Pseudotsuga* are generally resistant.
How to identify: Resin is exuded from the stems; growth stops; honey-coloured toadstools appear around the base of the tree and some way up its trunk in autumn.
Cause: Species of the fungus *Armillaria,* recognizable as black, bootlace-like strands underground.
Prevention: Not possible.
Control: Dig up and destroy any affected plants, then treat the soil with Armillatox.

Scale insects

Vulnerable plants: Most, but especially yew and members of Cupressaceae (*Chamaecyparis,* x *Cupressocyparis, Cupressus, Juniperus, Libocedrus, Metasequoia, Sequoia, Sequoiadendron, Taxodium* and *Thuja*).
How to identify: Usually oval, hard, scale-like insects cling to the stems; they leave a sticky deposit that encourages bacteria and fungi.
Prevention: Not usually possible.

Phytophthora infection, a soil-borne fungal disease.

Control: Remove low numbers on small conifers by hand. For larger infestations, spray with malathion, pirimiphos-methyl or a suitable insecticide in late spring to early summer.

Spruce aphid

Vulnerable plants: Mainly spruces.
How to identify: A woolly white deposit appears on stems and leaves.
Prevention: Not usually possible.
Control: Apply a spray of HCH in mid- to late winter or early summer.

Calendar

Spring

Plant new stock (container grown, root-balled and bare-root), both specimens and hedges. Protect young plants from frost and cold winds. Mulch new plantings. Pot on any seedlings that are large enough to handle. Pot on cuttings from the previous year, which should have rooted by late spring.

Pot on cuttings annually in spring until they are large enough to plant out.

Summer

During dry conditions mist the foliage of young plants not adapted to drought. Water new plantings during periods of prolonged drought. Clip hedges. Plant new stock (container-grown plants only). Take semi-ripe cuttings.

Clip over hedges in late spring and late summer. Leyland cypress requires trimming more frequently.

Autumn

Take cuttings. Plant new stock (container grown, root-balled and bare-root; mild areas only). Look out for honey fungus and take any remedial steps necessary. Mulch new plantings. Collect cones and extract seed for sowing.

Autumn is the time to collect conifer cones for seed or Christmas decoration. Any that are surplus can be burned.

Winter

Protect vulnerable trees from snow damage. Prune any conifers that need it. Replace leaders broken by storm damage or by other means. Cut out dead growth and tie in undamaged growth to cover it. Protect young trees from frost and cold winds.

Topiary specimens are a strong feature in a garden in winter. They look particularly impressive with a covering of snow.

Other recommended conifers

***Abies concolor* 'Argentea'** (syn. *A.c.* 'Candicans') Large, slim, conical conifer (the species from the USA to north Mexico) with needle-like, silver-blue leaves and blue or green cones. To 40m (approx.130ft) x 7m (23ft).
***Abies concolor* 'Compacta'** (syn. *A.c.* 'Glauca Compacta') Dwarf conifer (the species from the USA to northern Mexico) with upturned needle-like, silvery blue leaves and green or pale blue cones. 3m (10ft) x 3m (10ft).
Abies koreana (Korean fir) Small, conical conifer from Korea with needle-like dark green leaves (silver beneath) and striking, violet-blue cones. 10m (33ft) x 6m (20ft).
***Abies lasiocarpa* 'Roger Watson'** Dwarf conical conifer (the species from North America) with needle-like, silver-grey leaves; violet-blue cones. 1m (3ft) x 1m (3ft).

***Abies procera* 'Glauca'**

***Abies procera* 'Glauca'** Medium-sized, conical conifer (the species from the USA) with needle-like, glaucous blue leaves and purple-brown cones. Can be shrubby. 15m (approx. 50ft) x 7m (23ft).
Abies veitchii (Veitch fir) Large, slim, conical conifer from Japan with needle-like leaves that are dark green above and silvery-white beneath; the cones are violet blue. 20m (66ft) x 6m (20ft).
Araucaria araucana (Chilean pine, Monkey puzzle) Large, usually dioecious, conifer from Chile and Argentina that develops a broad, dome-shaped crown on a tall trunk. The distinctive bark is wrinkled and greyish brown. The leaves are roughly triangular and dark green; the cones are brown. 25m (82ft) x 10m (33ft).
Austrocedrus chilensis (syn. *Libocedrus chilensis*); (Chilean incense cedar) Medium-sized conical conifer from Chile and Argentina with scale-like dark green leaves and brown cones. 15m (approx. 50ft) x 4m (13ft).
Cedrus libani (Cedar of Lebanon) Large conical then spreading conifer from the Middle East with needle-like dark greyish green leaves and greyish pink cones. 30m (approx. 100ft) x 30m (approx. 100ft).
***Chamaecyparis lawsoniana* 'Intertexta'** Large, slim, conical conifer (the species from North America) with pendent, greyish green leaves. 20m (66ft) x 10m (33ft).
***Chamaecyparis lawsoniana* 'Minima'** Dwarf, rounded conifer (the species from North America) with scale-like, light green leaves and reddish brown male cones (the female insignificant). 1.5m (5ft) x 1m (3ft).
***Chamaecyparis obtusa* 'Nana Pyramidalis'** Dwarf, conical conifer (the species from Japan) with scale-like, dark green leaves and yellowish brown cones. 60cm (2ft) x 60cm (2ft).
Chamaecyparis thyoides (syn. *Cupressus thyoides*); (White cypress) Medium-sized, conical conifer from the USA with scale-like, bluish grey leaves; small, greyish blue cones. 15m (50ft) x 4m (13ft).

Cedrus libani

***Cryptomeria japonica* 'Pyramidata'** Small, columnar conifer (the species from Japan) with wedge-shaped leaves that are bluish green when young, ageing to dark green; the cones are brown. 4m (13ft) x 40cm (16in).

Cryptomeria japonica 'Sekka-sugi'

***Cryptomeria japonica* 'Sekka-sugi'** (syn. *C. j.* 'Cristata') Small, semi-weeping conifer (the species from Japan) with needle-like, light, greenish cream leaves and brown cones. 10m (33ft) x 4m (13ft).
Cunninghamia lanceolata (Chinese fir) Medium-sized, conical conifer from China with reddish brown, furrowed bark; needle-like, glossy green leaves and greenish brown cones. 20m (66ft) x 6m (20ft).
x *Cupressocyparis leylandii* 'Castlewellan' Large, columnar, hybrid conifer with

scale-like, burnished yellow leaves and dark brown cones. 25m (82ft) x 10m (33ft).
x ***Cupressocyparis leylandii* 'Harlequin'** Large, columnar, hybrid conifer with scale-like greyish leaves, marked white, and dark brown cones. 25m (82ft) x 10m (33ft).
Cupressus sempervirens (Italian cypress, Mediterranean cypress) Medium-sized, slim, columnar conifer from the Mediterranean and Iran with scale-like, greyish green leaves and greyish brown cones. 20m (66ft) x 6m (20ft).
***Cupressus torulosa* 'Cashmeriana'** (syn. *C. cashmeriana*; Kashmir cypress) Large, broadly conical conifer (possibly occurring wild in the Himalayas) with aromatic leaves on pendent stems; small cones mature dark brown. Not hardy. 30m (approx. 100ft) x 10m (33ft).
Fitzroya cupressoides (Patagonian cypress) Medium-sized, irregular conifer from Chile and Argentina. Reddish bark peels in long strips. Dark green leaves are lined with white; cones are light brown. 15m (approx. 50ft) x 6m (20ft).
Ginkgo biloba (Maidenhair tree) Large, deciduous, dioecious tree from China but now found only in gardens; not strictly a conifer, it is usually included among them. Columnar initially, it spreads with age. Fan-shaped, waxy, bright green leaves turn

Gingko biloba

brilliant yellow in autumn. Fruits are plum-like. 30m (approx. 100ft) x 8m (26ft).
***Juniperus chinensis* 'Keteleeri'** Medium-sized, columnar to conical conifer (the species from China, Mongolia and Japan) with scale-like, greyish green leaves; blue "berries" ripen with a paler bloom. 10m (33ft) x 2m (6½ft).
***Juniperus chinensis* 'Stricta'** Dwarf, conical conifer (the species from China, Mongolia and Japan) with both scale-like and needle-like bluish green leaves; the "berries" have a distinct white bloom. 2.5m (8ft) x 60cm (2ft).
***Juniperus* 'Grey Owl'** (syn. *J. virginiana* 'Grey Owl') Dwarf, spreading conifer with needle-

Juniperus virginiana 'Grey Owl'

like, silvery grey leaves and glaucous violet "berries". 3m (10ft) x 4m (13ft).
***Juniperus horizontalis* 'Douglasii'** Dwarf, creeping conifer (the species from North America) with bright green leaves flushed purple in winter, needle-like when young becoming scale-like with age, and dark blue "berries". 50cm (20in) x 2m (6½ft) or more.
Juniperus procumbens (Bonin Island juniper) Spreading conifer from Japan with reddish brown bark, needle-like, light green leaves and brown or black "berries". 75cm (30in) x 2m (6½ft).
***Juniperus sabina* 'Tamariscifolia'** Dwarf, spreading conifer (the species from central Europe to north China) with scale-like, blue-green leaves (flushing purple in winter) and blue-black "berries". 1m (3ft) x 2m (6½ft).
***Juniperus scopulorum* 'Springbank'** Dwarf, narrowly conical conifer (the species from the USA) with scale-like, silvery-blue leaves and blue "berries". 2m (6½ft) x 60cm (2ft).
***Juniperus squamata* 'Chinese Silver'** Dwarf, rather untidy, spreading conifer (the species from Afghanistan, the Himalayas and China) with needle-like, silvery-blue leaves and black "berries". 4m (13ft) x 4m (13ft).
***Juniperus virginiana* 'Burkii'** Small, columnar conifer (the species from the USA) with both scale-like and needle-like, glaucous green leaves that tinge purple in autumn; dark blue "berries" develop a lighter bloom as they ripen. 6m (20ft) x 1m (3ft).
Microbiota decussata Dwarf, spreading conifer from Russia with scale-like, yellowish green leaves that turn bronze in winter and yellowish brown cones. 1m (3ft) x 3m (10ft) or more.
Phyllocladus trichomanoides (Tanekaha) Medium-sized, rounded conifer from New Zealand with feather-like, dark green phylloclades (flattened stems that function as leaves) and catkin-like male cones that ripen from purple through red to yellow. Not hardy. 12m (40ft) x 6m (20ft).
Picea abies (Common spruce, Norway spruce) Large, conical conifer from north and central Europe with needle-like leaves and shiny brown

cones. Widely grown as a Christmas tree. 40m (approx. 130ft) x 6m (20ft).
Picea breweriana (Brewer spruce) Medium-sized, conical conifer from the USA. Horizontal branches have pendent branchlets with needle-like, bluish green leaves. Cones are purplish brown. 15m (approx. 50ft) x 4m (13ft).
Picea engelmannii (Engelmann spruce, Mountain spruce) Medium-sized, broadly conical conifer from North America; needle-like, glaucous green leaves and small purplish brown cones. 15m (approx. 50ft) x 4m (13ft).
***Picea glauca* 'Coerulea'** Medium-sized, conical conifer (the species from North America); needle-like, glaucous blue leaves, pale brown cones. 15m (approx. 50ft) x 6m (20ft).
***Picea mariana* 'Doumetii'** Small, broadly conical conifer (the species from North America) with needle-like, dark green leaves and purplish cones. 5m (16½ft) x 5m (16½ft)
***Picea mariana* 'Nana'** Dwarf, conical conifer (the species from North America); needle-like, bluish green leaves and dark greyish brown cones. 50cm (20in) x 50cm (20in).
Picea morrisonicola (Taiwan spruce) Medium-sized, conical to columnar conifer from Taiwan with needle-like, dark green leaves and purple cones. 15m (approx. 50ft) x 7m (23ft).
Pinus aristata (Bristle-cone pine) Small, conical conifer from the USA with long,

Pinus banksiana

needle-like, pale bluish green leaves and bristly brown cones. 10m (33ft) x 6m (20ft).
Pinus banksiana (Jack pine) Medium-sized, conical conifer from North America with paired, needle-like, bright green leaves and light brown cones. 20m (66ft) x 5m (16½ft).
Pinus bungeana (Lace-bark pine) Small, rounded conifer from China with flaking, grey-green bark, needle-like, dark green leaves and brown cones. 10m (33ft) x 6m (20ft).
Pinus cembra (Arolla pine, Swiss stone pine) Medium-sized, conical conifer from central Europe with long, needle-like, dark green leaves and bluish cones that ripen

Pinus jeffreyi

brown. 20m (66ft) x 8m (26ft).
Pinus cembroides (Mexican stone pine, Pinyon) Small, rounded conifer from the south USA and north Mexico with silver-grey bark, needle-like, dark green leaves and green cones. Not reliably hardy. 8m (26ft) x 5m (16½ft).
Pinus contorta (Beach pine, Shore pine) Medium-sized, conical to rounded conifer from North America with long, needle-like, bright green leaves and yellowish brown cones. 15m (approx. 50ft) x 8m (26ft).
Pinus coulteri (Big-cone pine, Coulter pine) Large conifer from the USA and Mexico; it develops a dome-like crown on a clear trunk. The needle-like, greyish green leaves are sparse; the large, yellow-brown cones are prickly. 25m (82ft) x 10m (33ft).
Pinus halepensis (Aleppo pine) Medium-sized, open, conical conifer from the Mediterranean with long, needle-like, bright green leaves and glossy brown cones. 20m (66ft) x 6m (20ft).
Pinus jeffreyi (Black pine, Jeffrey pine) Large, slim conifer from North America that develops a clear trunk. Bark is black and deeply fissured. Long, needle-like leaves are greyish green; cones are yellowish grey. 35m (115ft) x 8m (26ft).
Pinus leucodermis (Bosnian pine) Large, conical conifer from the Balkans with needle-like, dark green leaves and cones that ripen from blue to brown. 20m (66ft) x 6m (20ft).
***Pinus leucodermis* 'Compact Gem'** Dwarf, broadly conical conifer (the species from the Balkans) with needle-like, dark green leaves and blue, then brown, cones. 30cm (1ft) x 30cm (1ft).
Pinus montezumae (Montezuma pine, Rough-bark Mexican pine) Large conifer with a dome-shaped head from Mexico and Guatemala. The long, needle-like leaves are bluish grey; the cones are yellow or brown. Not reliably hardy. 30m (approx. 100ft) x 9m (30ft).
Pinus muricata (Bishop pine) Large, slim conifer with a domed crown from the USA. Long, needle-like leaves are bluish green; cones are light brown. 20m (66ft) x 9m (30ft).

Pinus parviflora (Japanese white pine) Medium-sized, conical but spreading conifer from Japan with needle-like, bluish green leaves and reddish brown cones. 20m (66ft) x 8m (26ft).
Pinus peuce (Macedonian pine) Large, narrowly columnar conifer from the Balkans and Greece with needle-like, greyish green leaves and green cones ripening to brown. 25m (82ft) x 8m (26ft).

Pinus peuce

Pinus pinea (Stone pine, Umbrella pine) Small conifer with a rounded crown on a clear trunk from the Mediterranean. Long, needle-like leaves are dark green and the cones are glossy brown. 20m (66ft) x 12m (approx. 40ft).
Pinus ponderosa (Western yellow pine) Large conifer, roughly columnar though upright-growing, that develops a clear trunk, from North America. Bark cracks into smooth, broad plates. Long, needle-like leaves are greyish green; cones are purple-brown. 35m (115ft) x 8m (26ft).
Pinus radiata (Monterey pine) Large, roughly conical conifer from the USA with needle-like, dark green leaves and yellowish brown cones. 40m (approx. 130ft) x 12m (approx. 40ft).
Pinus rigida (Northern pitch pine) Medium-sized, open, unevenly conical conifer from North America with needle-like, dark green leaves and reddish brown cones. 20m (66ft) x 7m (23ft).
Pinus strobus (Eastern white pine, Weymouth pine) Large conifer from North America with needle-like, greyish green leaves and light brown cones. 35m (115ft) x 8m (26ft).
***Pinus sylvestris* 'Doone Valley'** Dwarf, irregular conifer (the species from Europe and parts of Asia) with needle-like, bluish green leaves and grey- or red-brown cones. 1m (3ft) x 1m (3ft).
***Pinus sylvestris* 'Gold Coin'** Dwarf, conical conifer (the species from Europe and parts of Asia) with needle-like leaves that are bright golden yellow in winter and spring, bluish green for the rest of the year; cones are grey- or red-brown. 2m (6½ft) x 2m (6½ft).

Pinus radiata

***Pinus sylvestris* 'Fastigiata'** Small, columnar conifer (the species from Europe and Asia) with needle-like, bluish green leaves and grey- or red-brown cones. 8m (26ft) x 3m (10ft).
Pinus thunbergii (Japanese black pine) Medium-sized conifer with a domed head and a clear trunk, from China, Japan and Korea with long, needle-like, dark green leaves and greyish brown cones. 25m (82ft) x 8m (26ft).
Pinus virginiana (Scrub pine, Virginia pine) Medium-sized conifer with an irregularly shaped head on a tall trunk, from the USA. Long, needle-like leaves are yellowish or grey green; cones, red-brown. 15m (approx. 50ft) x 8m (26ft).
Pinus wallichiana (Bhutan pine, Himalayan pine) Large, broadly conical conifer from the Himalayas; drooping grey-green leaves; brown cones. 35m (115ft) x 12m (approx. 40ft).
Podocarpus nivalis (Alpine totara) Dwarf, rounded conifer from New Zealand with linear, bronze-green leaves and red fruits. 2m (6½ft) x 2m (6½ft).
Podocarpus salignus (Willowleaf podocarp) Medium-sized, dioecious, conical conifer from Chile with long, willow-like, light green leaves and peeling red-brown bark. Female trees produce deep violet fruits. 20m (66ft) x 9m (30ft).
***Pseudotsuga menziesii* 'Fretsii'** Dwarf, conical conifer (the species from North America) with needle-like, dull green leaves and brown cones. 6m (20ft) x 4m (13ft) but slow-growing.
***Thuja occidentalis* 'Caespitosa'** Dwarf, rounded conifer (the species from North America) with scale-like, yellowish green leaves and brown cones. 30cm (1ft) x 40cm (16in).
***Thuja occidentalis* 'Smaragd'** Dwarf, conical conifer (the species from North America) with scale-like, bright green leaves and brown cones. 1m (3ft) x 1m (3ft).
***Thuja plicata* 'Collyer's Gold'** Dwarf, conical conifer (the species from North America) with scale-like leaves, bright yellow in spring, turning light green; brown cones. 2m (6½ft) x 1m (3ft).

Index

***Thuja plicata* 'Hillieri'** Dwarf, rounded conifer (the species from North America) with scale-like, bright green leaves and brown cones. 2m (6½ft) x 2m (6½ft).

***Thujopsis dolabrata* 'Variegata'** Small, conical conifer (the species from Japan) with scale-like, dark green leaves marked with creamy-white and brown cones. 10m (33ft) x 4m (13ft).

Torreya californica (California nutmeg) Medium-sized, roughly conical conifer from the USA with needle-like, glossy green leaves and olive-like fruits. 25m (82ft) x 8m (26ft).

Tsuga canadensis

Tsuga canadensis (Canada hemlock, Eastern hemlock) Medium-sized, roughly conical conifer from North America with needle-like, two-ranked, dark green leaves and pale brown cones. 25m (80ft) x 10m (30ft).

ACKNOWLEDGEMENTS

The publisher would like to thank the following for their assistance in the preparation of this book: Bedgebury National Pinetum, Bedgebury, East Sussex; Beeches Nurseries, Radclive, Buckingham; Buckingham Nurseries, Buckingham; Mr and Mrs A. Keech, Long Buckby, Northants; Mrs J. Hurry and Mr S. Hurry, Long Buckby, Northants; Sir Harold Hillier Gardens and Arboretum, Ampfield, Hants. All the photographs in this book were taken by Peter Anderson, with the exception of the following: Peter McHoy: p52 (br), 57 (l & r), 58 (cb), 59 (l & r), 60, 61, 62; Harry Smith Collection: 56 (l & r), 59 (c), 63 (l).